SIGNPOSTS
TO SPELLING

Heinemann Educational Books Ltd
Halley Court, Jordan Hill, Oxford OX2 8EJ

OXFORD LONDON EDINBURGH
MELBOURNE SYDNEY AUCKLAND
IBADAN NAIROBI GABORONE HARARE
KINGSTON PORTSMOUTH NH (USA)
SINGAPORE MADRID

First published 1978 by the
Helen Arkell Dyslexia Centre (H.A.D.C.)
14 Crondace Road, London SW6 4BB

This revised edition published 1980 by
Heinemann Educational Books Ltd
Reprinted 1981, 1983, 1988, 1990

ISBN 0 435 10686 4

Printed in Great Britain by
Richard Clay Ltd, Bungay, Suffolk

Designed by J. Elsegood

Contents

Preface 5

SPELLING GUIDES

Short Vowels 8

After a short vowel, double the consonant. 10

Long Vowels and Silent E 12

Flossy Words 13

I, Y and E soften C and G 14

All, Full and Till 16

C, K or CK? 17

Suffix ING 18

Y 20

Suffix ED, D or T? 22

Words ending in LE 24

Suffixes able and ible 26

TCH 28

DGE 29

Suffix ly 30

I before E except after C 31

Suffix tion 32

Plurals 34

W 36

O or U 37

DAYS OF THE WEEK 38

HELPFUL HINTS 39

THE ENGLISH LANGUAGE 44

CONCLUSION 57

Suggestions for further reading 60

.... MORE LOGIC THAN AT FIRST APPEARS

Preface

This book is intended for teachers—in class, in remedial sessions, and teaching English to foreigners—so that they may give their pupils the kind of insight into the English language that will help them to improve their spelling. It is designed to give quick and easy reference to the information. As the need for any spelling guide arises in the course of teaching, it can be found and explained to the pupil without delay. On some pages there are mnemonics and nonsense dictations as examples of what can be given to reinforce a particular guide. Some information on the history of the English language has been included on a question and answer basis. This is an important adjunct to the teaching of our spelling.

There are various reasons why some people are poor spellers. Perhaps the most common is that they have difficulty in reading (or may merely be disinclined to read), and it is almost impossible to spell a word correctly that one has never seen. However, even those who read with ease may not be able to recall the mental picture of a word when they want to write it down. These are people who have poor visual perception for symbols. They are therefore unable to take accurate mental photographs of words, which good spellers do automatically. Good spellers store away these images in their minds. When writing, they draw the required word from this store and write down what they see in their mind's eye. For those whose mental photographs for words are either blurred or non-existent, the apparent illogicality of English spelling can arouse feelings of despair and humiliation. It is with the view of mitigating such feelings and of showing that there is more logic in our spelling than at first appears that this book has been written.

The term *spelling guide* has been used rather than spelling rule, as the latter implies that it is foolproof. There are nearly always exceptions and often many of them. As most pupils will be labouring under difficulties, it smoothes their path to present guidelines which are relevant to a high percentage of words. The examples of words following a guide do not form a comprehensive list. Such lists would be daunting for both teacher and pupil. Rather is this an attempt to simplify as much as possible the complexities of English spelling and to present its basic structure in the form of guides, which have proved to be the most useful to the author after many years' experience in teaching poor spellers. In the course of studying these guides it will be seen that English spelling is much more rational than most people realise.

Preface

Teachers often ask in what order information on phonics and spelling guides should be presented. Ideally, one should present what is most appropriate for a pupil in any lesson. However, whatever the order, all pupils should learn at an early stage the difference between short and long vowels. Many guides are based on their distinction. Hence guide 1 deals with short vowels.

Short vowels and consonant sounds are denoted by lower-case letters, long vowels and consonant names are shown by upper-case letters.

A teacher should provide first a spelling guide or other information when the occasion arises, and then give mnemonics and dictations which include words such as those in the lists of examples. In this way a pupil gradually assimilates the guide in question. These activities may be lightened by games. A few suggestions have been made under *Things to do* (i.e. for the pupil to do) and teachers will no doubt introduce others of their own. Inevitably it will be a gradual process. Even when he[1] appears to have assimilated a guide in a remedial session mistakes will occur when he is more off-guard while writing in class. Much help and encouragement will be needed from the teacher, and a great deal of reinforcement, until correct spelling becomes more automatic.

Nonsense dictations provide a humorous element in remedial lessons. Dictations are considered to be a chore and anything that can be done to alleviate the dullness of the task will be welcomed. Only mistakes in words that have already been covered by the guides should be rectified, as a mass of corrections cannot be digested all at once and will merely lead to the pupil becoming depressed. Class teachers should be encouraged to cooperate with remedial teachers. In this way they will be aware of what has been learnt in remedial sessions, and will then be able to look out for opportunities to reinforce the guides in class. At the same time they will make allowances for mis-spellings in words of guides yet to be tackled.

It is expected that a pupil in a remedial class will be already learning phonics as a basis for these spelling guides. Although ideas have been given for introducing each guide, most pupils will need to be given

---

[1] To facilitate reading, teachers are referred to in the feminine and pupils in the masculine throughout this book.

Preface

further detailed instruction and practice by using equipment to reinforce a guide. The following equipment, often used in centres for
teaching the perceptually handicapped and dyslexics, is to be
recommended: The Edith Norrie Letter-Case, The Pictogram System, and
The Gillingham-Stillman Course.[2] (There are a number of adaptations
of the original Gillingham-Stillman Course, including a recent comprehensive adaptation by Kathleen Hickey.) Also found to be useful are
the phonic and remedial programmes that go with the Tutorpack
teaching machine,[3] as well as the Stott Programmed Reading Kit.[4]
Both of these are attractive and stimulating material.

It is up to the teacher to judge what information will be most helpful
to her pupil at any given time, depending on his age, intelligence, etc.
She should then select a point to be digested, discarding exceptions
until he is ready to absorb more. It is unrealistic to expect poor spellers
to take in *all* the information in these spelling guides. Selection, to meet
their individual needs, is essential.

It should be stressed that this is a *teacher's* handbook. Neither child
nor adult should be expected to teach himself from it. Both will need
direction and tuition from an experienced and sympathetic teacher,
for improving spelling to an acceptable standard is a hard grind, which
those able to spell with ease usually have difficulty in understanding.
Nevertheless, when a pupil has *finished* a course on spelling, he might
well find it useful to have a copy of this book to hand for reference.

[2] For information on this equipment write to the following:

The Edith Norrie Letter-Case: H.A.D.C., 14 Crondace Road, London SW6 4BB
The Pictogram System: Pictogram Supplies, Barton, Cambridge CB3 7AY
The Gillingham-Stillman Equipment: Better Books, 11 Springfield Place,
Lansdowne Road, Bath, Avon BA1 5RA

[3] Where appropriate, reference is made to these programmes after the guides.
For further information on the Tutorpack write to: H.A.D.C., 14 Crondace Road,
London SW6 4BB

[4] For information on the Stott Programmed Reading Kit write to:
Holmes McDougall Ltd., Allander House, 137-141 Leith Walk, Edinburgh
EH6 8Ns, Scotland

SPELLING GUIDES

1 Short Vowels

Discrimination between the short vowels often causes great problems because their sounds differ so little from each other.

A Clue Card, such as the one illustrated below, provides a useful mnemonic for these sounds.[1] Get the pupil to make his own and keep it by him. When, for instance, he has difficulty in discriminating

between e and i,[2] the pictures of the egg and igloo give the clue. The two words should be said aloud, listening carefully to each initial sound. If he has written peg for pig, the teacher says *pig*, then **p**, and encourages him to respond with the vowel-sound which follows—in this case i. Looking at the Clue Card, he will then link i with igloo and see at once which vowel he wants.

8

_a e i o u_

Things to do:

i. _Write down, or put out on the table, two or more vowels. Ask the pupil to point to the letter-sound he hears in some of the following words: at, in, up, on, ant, end, bit, rat, pot, cut, bad, red, bat, hit, met, lot, sit, set, got, get, hut, men, van, log, sum, rub, man, then, thin, dog, cat, fish, gun, pat, sun, pen, run, bed, rod, etc._

ii. _Place vowel finger-puppets on five of the child's fingers. Tell a short story, asking him to raise the appropriate puppet as he hears the short vowel-sounds. If no puppets are available, write the vowels on his nails with a felt pen. The ink is easily washed off afterwards._

iii. _Isolate short vowel-sounds (which is necessary when writing) by train-ing the automatic response, e.g. Say_ dog - **d**, _and the pupil responds with_ **o**.

N.B. **Y** acts as a short vowel when it has the sound **i**, as in Mummy, puppy, family. (It acts as a long vowel when it has the sound **I**.) It follows that every word has at least one vowel. Polysyllabic words have at least one vowel in each syllable.

Many of the following guides refer to short vowel-sounds, so it is im-portant that these are known. If a pupil has particular difficulty in their discrimination, he should keep a Clue Card to hand for reference. A teacher may then go on to other spelling guides, while he is still getting practice in guide number 1.

[1] The pronunciation of English varies, not only in different parts of the United Kingdom, but in different parts of the world. This applies especially to vowel-sounds. If need be, a teacher should provide other examples of words that suit the speech of her pupil.

[2] Remember that short vowels and consonant sounds are indicated by lower-case letters. Long vowels and consonant names are shown by upper-case letters.

2 "After a short vowel, double the consonant. Double the what? The Con-son-ant."

This guide applies to words of more than one syllable. It is a very general guide which serves as a useful reminder in a large number of words. Compare the following: *dinner/diner; hopping/hoping; tapping/taping.* This doubling of the consonant prevents the second vowel from making the first vowel long. (See guide 3.)

N.B. **K** is not doubled, write **CK** instead. Compare backing/baking.

(It should be noted that this rule does not apply to Latin- and Greek-derived words. Therefore, teachers should be judicious about its use by an older student with a wide vocabulary.)

Daddy	better	dinner	lorry	Mummy
Granny	letter	silly	sorry	hurry
happy	penny	skipping	poppy	sunny
rabbit	yellow	swimmer	follow	supper
blacker	beckon	chicken	pocket	lucky
jacket	pecking	kicking	rocket	plucking
packet	wrecker	cricket	stocking	mucky
cracking	checking	sticky	locking	clucking

(N.B. soccer, tobacco, Piccadilly)

plan — planning — planned
stop — stopping — stopped

big — bigger — biggest
red — redder — reddest

N.B. i. **X** is never doubled; it has in any case two sounds, **ks**.
ii. **V** is not doubled; exceptions— *navvy, skivvy* (though these should not be mentioned to the pupil who is being introduced to guide 2.)

Dictation: Silly Sally sent her Granny a kipper in a letter. The unhappy
   postman had to hurry with the packet.

Things to do:
*Draw Silly Sally . . . and the kipper . . . then Granny getting the letter.
Write their names by them.*
*Now think of more words that double the consonant after a short
vowel.*
At this point the teacher should check that the pupil has remembered
the **CK** words.

For more lists of words see Gill Cotterell's Phonic Reference Cards, published
by Language Development Aids, Park Works (B), Norwich Road, Wisbech,
Cambridgeshire PE13 2AX.
Also useful for word-lists is the book *Learning to Spell* by Irene Martyn,
published by Harper of Holloway.

3 Long Vowels and Silent E

Silent E makes the preceding vowel say its name, if there is only one consonant between them. This is an important guide and should be explained particularly carefully. The following words may be used to give plenty of practice:

mat—mate	pet—Pete	kit—kite	hop—hope	us—use
fat—fate	them—theme	rip—ripe	cod—code	cub—cube
gap—gape		pip—pipe	not—note	tub—tube
hat—hate		fin—fine	rob—robe	plum—plume
mad—made		win—wine	rod—rode	
rat—rate		bit—bite		
at—ate		slim—slime		

 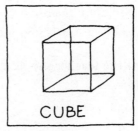

N.B. Silent E does not necessarily have to come at the end of a word—
Peter, paper, driver, makes, used, etc.

Guide 3 can be taken a stage further: other vowels also lengthen the preceding vowel when there is only one consonant between them.

hating	remedial	riding	solar	tubular
basin	competing	tidy	notable	music

N.B. Y acts as a long vowel in words such as my, fly, cry.

As with guide 2 this is a useful general guide. Some common exceptions are:

ever	seven	any	family	panic
never	eleven	many		
clever				

Remember—Never double **V**!

Dictation: Pete's pet made me mad. I hate her hat!

Flossy Words

Words of one syllable ending in **F**, **L** or **S** (hence FLOSSY) double that
letter after a short vowel:

staff	Jeff	stiff	off	cuff
shall	yell	will	doll	fuss
ass	mess	kiss	cross	pull (u = short oo)

Exceptions: of if us pal gas bus yes

Dictation: The Swiss miss sent a kiss to the gruff man as he fell with a
yell off the cliff.

Things to do:
Think of a word that rhymes with **fell**. *How will it end? Write it down.
Can you think of any more? (bell, dell, hell, Nell, sell, tell, well, yell,
shell, spell, swell). What does* **gruff** *mean? Think of a word that rhymes
with it. (buff, cuff, fluff, huff, muff, puff, stuff, scruff).*
If pupils produce words like *enough, rough, tough,* tell them that these
are **special** words. Judge whether or not they are able to understand
that **gh** was at one time a guttural sound. If they are, tell them and
demonstrate. Next lesson, ask pupils if they remember any Flossy
Rhyming Words. Remind them, find more words, and continue the
process.

5 I, Y and E soften C and G

Compare: Hard C –cat, cot, cut   Soft C (s) – face, city, cycle
         Hard G –gang, got, gun   Soft G (j) – gentle, giant, energy

ce	ice	**ci**	city	**cy**	cycle
	cell		civilian		cygnet
	certain		pencil		cyclamen
	place		racing		Lucy
	centre		citizen		Percy
	office		circus		

Dictation: Percy the cygnet raced round the circus ring.

ge	age	**gi**	giant	**gy**	energy
	refuge		ginger		orgy
	dungeon		gipsy		podgy
	gem		magic		biology
	danger		agitate		sociology
	gentle		giraffe		gymnastics

Dictation: Down in the city centre gipsies were driving giraffes to the circus. Citizens, hurrying to their offices, had to take refuge in garages and cinemas and other strange places. Some even plunged into a nearby dungeon where, to their amazement, they saw a giant in a cell eating iced ginger.

Things to do:

*i. Underline words with soft **c** in red and those with soft **g** in blue, using the dictation opposite or other appropriate text.*

*ii. Look up in a dictionary more words beginning with **ce, ci, cy,** and **ge, gi, gy**.*

N.B. There are exceptions such as *get, give, girl, begin.* These words are often already known to pupils before they are given this guide. Consequently they seldom notice that they *are* exceptions. In which case, do not mention it!

N.B. In some words **U** is inserted after **G** to keep the sound hard:

guide	guess	league
guilt	guest	colleague
guilty		rogue
guitar		synagogue
disguise		catalogue

Dictation: Guess who is the guest with the big guitar.
He is right by the guide with the Jaguar.

No English word ends in either **V** or **J**.

No English word ends in **I** except tax*i*, which in any case is short for *taximeter cab.*

15

6 All, Full and Till

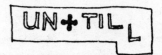

When *all, full* and *till* are joined to a word or syllable, they drop an **L**:

a.   all

also	altogether
always	although
almost	almighty
already	alright (all right *is better English*)

b.   full

hopeful	dreadful	fulfil
grateful	frightful	fulsome
shameful	helpful	
joyful	painful	

c.   till   until

Dictation: He is always awful until all his tills are full.

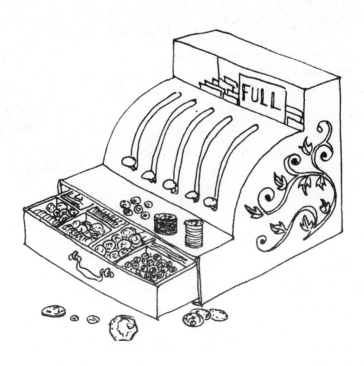

C, K or CK?   7

a. Write **C** if followed by **A, O, U**, or a consonant:

cat	cot	cut	clan	crest	act
can	cod	cub	cling	crab	pact

Dictation: The family crest of the clan is a cat in a cot.

b. Write **K** if hard **k** is followed by **E or I**:

kennel	king	keep	kite
Kenneth	kitten	keen	kind
lake	bike	awoke	Luke
rake	Mike	broke	duke

Exceptions: *kangaroo* (a word which possibly came from the aborigines in Australia), *skate, skull*

Dictation: King Mike was playing poker
With a duke and a stoker
By the kennel sat kind Jake
Trying hard to keep awake.
And Lucy—that dear lady! —
Was being kissed by Luke O'Grady.
"That's just life!"
Joked O'Grady's wife.

c. Write **CK** after a short vowel: (Guide 2)

sack	speck	sick	shock	duck
shack	neck	tricky	rocky	plucky

Exceptions: multi-syllabic words ending in *ic*

traffic	terrific	Atlantic
panic	picnic	Pacific

Dictation: Kenneth keeps a panic-stricken
cuckoo in his pocket.

8 Suffix ING

Many words are made up of a prefix, stem and suffix. The letters (syllable) *fixed* on to the beginning of a stem are called prefix, and those *fixed* on to the end of the stem are the suffix:

turn (stem)   re-turn (prefix, stem)   re-turn-ing (prefix, stem, suffix)

When the action of a verb is continuous, we add the suffix *ing* to the stem of the verb. *I am reading* implies that the reading has not yet stopped.

Think of some action words (verbs) ending in **ing**.

The stem is sometimes modified when *ing* is added —

a. Some words where the stem does *not* change are:

| talk-ing | eat-ing | try-ing | catch-ing | fish-ing |
| sleep-ing | teach-ing | cry-ing | stretch-ing | wash-ing |

b. After a short vowel double the consonant before adding *ing*:

(Guide 2)

plan—planning   bet—betting   dig—digging
        shop—shopping   run—running

N.B. *beginning* needs plenty of practice.

c. If a verb ends in E, take off the E before adding *ing*:   (Guide 3)
take—taking   complete—completing   ride—riding
        hope—hoping   rule—ruling

N.B. Words ending in **EE** do not drop an **E**:   *seeing, fleeing, agreeing*

d. If a word ends in **IE**, change **IE** to **Y** before adding *ing*:
die—dying   tie—tying   lie—lying

N.B. Words already ending in **Y** merely add *ing: replying, allying, ferrying, hurrying, carrying, annoying.* These need plenty of practice.   (Guide 9)

Dictation: Jack was sitting on a rock waiting for his friend, Mike, who
was swimming in the sea. His sister was trying to count the
crabs which were scurrying along the shore before hiding
under rocks. She was beginning to lift up a rock when a crab
nipped her big toe. She fled screaming back to Jack, but he
just sat there grinning at her. What a brother!

Tutorpack ENS3

In all words be sure to write at least one vowel in each syllable.
(Guides 1 & 16)

Y usually comes at the end of a word. When a suffix is added, change
Y to I:

carry—carries—carried
hurry—hurries—hurried
reply—replies—replied
supply—supplies—supplied
deny—denies—denied
study—studies—studied

baby—babies   (Guide 17 ci & cii)
lady—ladies
body—bodies
seventy—seventies

mercy—merciless

happy—happily
easy—easily—easiness
lazy—lazily—laziness
steady—steadily—steadiness

rely—reliable

N.B. *Holiday* is derived from *holy day*, where Y has changed to I with
the addition of *day*. For this reason the L is not doubled after
the short vowel. Likewise, *business* comes from *busy + ness*.

When the suffix *ing* is added to a word ending in Y, the Y remains.
Careful listening will enable a pupil to realise that there are 3 syllables
in, for instance, carr-y-ing Consequently the Y is necessary. It forms
the second syllable.   (Guide 8)

hurrying	scurrying	bullying	ferrying	tarrying
marrying	dallying	harrying	rallying	worrying

The vowel combination *ii* only occurs in *taxiing* and *skiing*, the latter
being coined from the Scandinavian *ski + ing*.

Dictation: Seventy old ladies were happily carrying on illegal business
while on holiday in Italy.

10 Suffix ED, D or T?

Most verbs in the past tense end in ED, D or T. This guide shows which ending to choose.

a. If a word makes sense without the suffix, there must be an ED ending. (When the stem ends in E, the addition of D makes ED.)

walk–walked	hope–hoped
climb–climbed	promise–promised
follow–followed	shape–shaped

N.B. After a short vowel double the consonant. (Guide 2)
   This prevents the E of the suffix from making the vowel long.
   The same applies to the murmuring vowels: *ar, er, ir, ur* (not *or*)

hop–hopped	tar–tarred	N.B. bore–bored
rob–robbed	refer–referred	store–stored
pat–patted	stir–stirred	
scan–scanned	occur–occurred	

Exceptions to doubling the consonant: multi-syllabic words where the stress is not on the last syllable:

lengthen–lengthened	power–powered
abandon–abandoned	consider–considered

N.B. Words ending in L — after a short vowel — double the consonant regardless of accent:

compel–compelled	tunnel–tunnelled
quarrel–quarrelled	bedevil–bedevilled

b. If a word does not make sense without the suffix, add d or t, whichever sound is heard:

hel–d	kep–t
foun–d	crep–t
hear–d (pronounced **her**)	fel–t
sai–d (pronounced **se**)	ben–t

Exceptions: paid   spelt (also spelled)
           laid   dwelt (dwelled)
                          burnt (burned)

Put simply: Ask "Can I do this? " or "Can it happen? " If the answer
is "yes", the verb ends in **ED**. If "no", it ends in **D** or **T**.
e.g. Can I walk? Yes. Add **ED**: walked
Can I kep? No. Add the letter one hears, which is **t**: kept

One way to sort out *b* and *d*.

11 Words ending in LE

These words originally ended in **EL**. In Middle English the word *little* was written as *littel* -the **T** was doubled to prevent the **E** from lengthening the vowel. With the French influence on our language (where the pronunciation was lə rather than əl) native words, such as little as well as French-derived words were often written with **LE**. So it became litt*le* and tread*le*, along with French words such as *sensible, example, article, miracle.*

There are still some words ending in **EL** (tunnel, funnel, enamel, model, travel), some words ending in **AL** (pedal, medal, metal, opal), and some in **IL** (pupil, evil, daffodil, April), but by far the majority in this group end in **LE**. Therefore, when in doubt, choose **LE**!

(This group should not be confused with the group of adjectives formed by adding the suffix **AL** -natural, universal, effectual, etc.)

a. After a short vowel double the consonant, then add **LE**:

battle	settle	ripple	topple	muddle
gabble	kettle	riddle	hobble	struggle
saddle	nettle	middle	bottle	bubble
straggle	mettle	giggle	toggle	tussle
straddle	embezzle	scribble	nobble	truffle
dazzle			throttle	puzzle

When the sound is **k**, write **CK**:

tackle	heckle	tickle	cockles	buckle
crackle	freckle	pickle		chuckle

N.B. i. No letters are doubled if there are already two consonants:

stumble bundle gargle bangle bungle bawble

ii. A number of words end in **STLE** (not **SSLE**):

castle	wrestle	whistle	jostle	hustle
	trestle	bristle	apostle	bustle
		thistle		
		gristle		

(*Muscle* is derived from the Latin *musculus*, a little mouse. This is what a muscle resembles when it is drawn: hence mus*cle*.)

b. After a long vowel only one consonant is needed before adding **LE**:

able	beetle	bridle	noble	bugle	poodle
gable	steeple	bible	ogle		
stable	(people)	rifle			
ladle		trifle			

Dictation: A noble stumbled over a beetle as he hobbled to the stable with a saddle and a bridle.

Things to do:
*Listen to the word battle. Is the vowel long or short? How many **T**s will you write? Now what about the word nettle?. . . And rifle? What letters come after the vowel in tackle? In an exercise book make two columns, heading one* short vowel *and the other* long vowel. *Write the following words in the correct column: riddle, bridle, stable, bottle, gobble, bugle, nettle, struggle, steeple, able, tackle, haggle, table, paddle, tickle, grapple, rifle, apple, etc. What does gobble mean? . . . And haggle? . . . And ogle?*

Poor spellers especially are confused about the meanings of words. Take opportunities to discuss meanings of words and extend a pupil's vocabulary. From time to time check that this guide has been remembered.

Keep checking until it is used automatically.

12 Suffixes able and ible

The meaning of these suffixes is *able to* or *fit for*. (The more common spelling is *able*.)

a. i. *able* is added to a whole word:

accept-able
understand-able

change-able)   The E is needed after C and G when these
notice-able)   consonants are softened.   (Guide 5)

lov-able   ) The E is not needed, so is dropped.
un-believ-able)

justifi-able) Y changes to I before adding a suffix.   (Guide 9)
reli-able   )

N.B. *Probable* is *prove-able*, and therefore ends in *able*.

ii. When the stem ends in a **k** sound; add *able* (otherwise **C** would be softened by the **I** of *ible*):

despic-able	irrevoc-able	amic-able	extric-able
practic-able	multiplic-able	applic-able	implac-able
educ-able	communic-able	explic-able	impecc-able

b. i. *ible* is added when the stem does *not* form a whole word:

ed-ible	compat-ible	vis-ible	poss-ible
cred-ible	percept-ible	deris-ible	permiss-ible
	recept-ible	divis-ible	
		comprehens-ible	
		reprehens-ible	
		ostens-ible	

enforc-ible) The I of *ible* keeps the C soft.
invinc-ible)

tang-ible   ) The I of *ible* keeps the G soft.
neglig-ible   )
incorrig-ible)

N.B. Most exceptions to guide *a.i.* end in **S** or **T**:

sens-ible	corrupt-ible
respons-ible	destruct-ible
collaps-ible	contempt-ible
defens-ible	perfect-ible

Dictation: It was possible, even probable, that the incredible behaviour of the spy had been very noticeable. It was unbelievable that he could have thought the secret map to be edible.

Tutorpack ENS 4

13 TCH

After a short vowel put **T** before **CH**:

catch	fetch	ditch	Scotch	Dutch
match	stretch	pitch	hotch	hutch
hatch	ketchup	kitchen	potch	butcher (u = short oo)

Mnemonics: The *cat* is *cat*ching mice in the kitchen.
A *Scot* was drinking *Scot*ch.

Exceptions:

much	rich	ostrich	duchess
such	which	attach	bachelor
			sandwich

Dictation: "Look! There's such a nice ostrich attached to that tree," said the bachelor to the rich duchess.

After a short vowel put **D** before **GE**. (Double **G** would be hard.)

badge	edge	ridge	dodge	fudge
cadge	hedge	bridge	lodger	judge
Madge	ledge	fridge	podgy	nudge

Mnemonic: The *bad bad*ger is sitting on the edge of a ledge eating fudge.

N.B. i No **D** is needed if another consonant is present: *plunge, bulge*

   ii The **A** is long in **NGE** -words: *range, stranger, change, danger, angel*

Exceptions occur in multi-syllabic words ending in *age* and *ege*:

village	college
cottage	allege
garage	sacrilege
garbage	

15 Suffix ly

The suffix *ly* means *having the appearance of. Ghastly* originally meant *having the appearance of a ghost.*

LY is added to a *whole* word, and this determines whether there is one **L** or two in the word:

love-ly	general-ly
stupid-ly	final-ly
immediate-ly	grateful-ly
fortunate-ly	especial-ly
	financial-ly

Exceptions occur when a final **E** makes pronunciation difficult:

simple–simply	probable–probably
miserable–miserably	possible–possibly

N.B. shabby– shabb*i*ly   ready–read*i*ly   (Guide 9)
       crazy–craz*i*ly   steady–stead*i*ly

Two word-derivations which facilitate spelling:

interest   = *inter* + *est*: literally, *it is between*, i.e. something which comes between you and what you are doing catches your *interest.*

immediate = *im* + *mediate*: literally, *not in the middle or between*, i.e. not letting anything come between, and therefore doing something *immediately.*

I before E except after C – whenever it rhymes with *me*

I before E	except after C
chief	ceiling
field	deceive
yield	receive
shield	deceit
siege	receipt
priest	perceive
believe	conceive
piece	conceit

Mnemonic: A *piec*e of *pie*

Exceptions: seize, protein, Sheila, Keith, Neil

N.B. For some people, depending on their pronunciation, *either* and *neither* are exceptions.

The following are not exceptions, but are worth noting:

weight	eight	veil	leisure	their
height	eighteen	vein		heir
	eighty	rein		
		reign		

Mnemonic: *I* to the *end* will be a fr-*i*-end

Tutorpack ENS2

17 Suffix tion

This suffix is derived through French from Latin. In English **TION** is pronounced *shun*.

Where a *shun* sound occurs, *never* write **SH** except in *fashion* and *cushion*. Other possibilities for *shun* are **SION, SIAN. CION, CIAN,** and **CEAN.** However, approximately 85% of these words end in **TION.** Therefore, when in doubt choose **TION!**

nation	completion	addition	motion	pollution
operation	depletion	ignition	locomotion	institution
frustration		edition	notion	restitution
elation		recognition	lotion	devolution
station		competition	commotion	absolution
invitation		supposition	potion	solution
education		repetition	devotion	retribution
examination		condition		diminution

N.B. Only **I** has a short vowel-sound before **TION**; **A, E, O** and **U** are long.

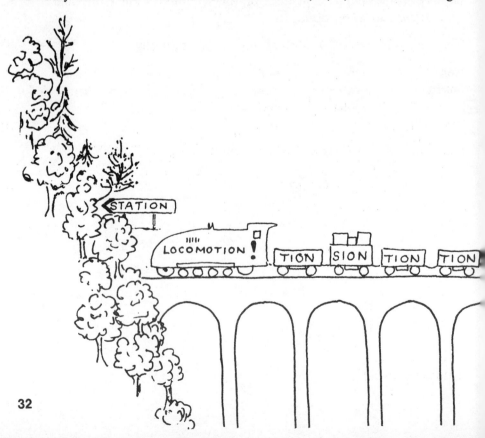

Some more **TION** words:

mention	section	question	corruption	portion
attention	election	suggestion	interruption	distortion
intention	fraction		eruption	
invention	action		gumption	
	attraction			distinction
	construction			junction
	perfection			function

N.B. Never use **K** in a *shun* word. These are Latin-derived words and there is no **K** in that language.

Things to do:

As these shun *words are often of 4 or 5 syllables, it is helpful to train the pupil to tap out, and count, the number of syllables in a word. Then he must be sure to have at least one vowel in each syllable. This prevents foreshortening words, which is a common fault.*

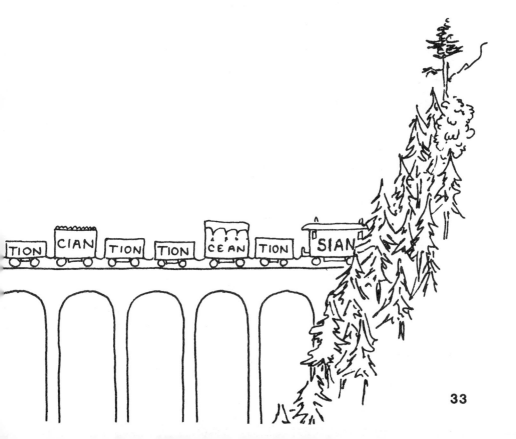

18 Plurals

It is important to check that the pupil understands that plural means *more than one* of anything. In English there are a variety of ways of making nouns plural:

a. The most common way is to add **S**:

dog—dogs
car—cars
book—books

N.B. Most words ending in **O** add **S** only.

Exceptions:

potato—potatoes   negro—negroes   volcano—volcanoes
tomato—tomatoes   echo—echoes   torpedo—torpedoes
cargo—cargoes   hero—heroes   mosquito—mosquitoes

b. Words ending in **SS, SH, CH, X** add **ES**:

dress—dresses   dish—dishes   witch—witches   fox—foxes
ass—asses   wish—wishes   ditch—ditches   box—boxes

N.B. Listening for the last syllable reminds the pupil that **ES** is needed.

c. i Words ending in a consonant + **Y**, change **Y** to **I** and add **ES**:

ruby—rubies   puppy—puppies   (Guide 9)
party—parties   story—stories
family—families   pony—ponies

ii. Words ending in a vowel + **Y**, add **S**:

valley—valleys   day—days
key—keys   boy—boys
monkey—monkeys   toy—toys

d. Many words ending in **F**, change **F** to **V** and add **ES**:

leaf—leaves   knife—knives   wife—wives
self—selves   life—lives   wolf—wolves

N.B. The ending of these words is in accordance with their sound.

There are other ways of forming plurals, but usually the sound-pattern
is a guide to the spelling:

mice	feet	children (**EN** is an Old English plural)
	teeth	oxen
	geese	brethren

N.B. The plural of *man* is *men*. It follows that the plural of *woman*
   (originally *wife-man*) is *wo-***men.**

Tutorpack ENG3

a. **W** changes **a** to **o**, and **ar** to **or**:

was	wasp	(water)	war	warrant	swan
want	wander		warm	wattle	swallow
wash	Walter		wart		swarm
watch	Wanda		warble		swarthy

N.B. **QU** makes the sound **kw**, and also changes **a** to **o**:

qualify	squash
quality	squad
quantity	squander
quarter	squabble

b. **W** changes **o** to **u**, and **or** to **ur**:

won	work	worm
wonder	word	worth
worry	world	worse

Dictations: i. Walter the wasp was watching a swan on the water,
When down came a swallow and squashed flat his daughter.

ii. Walter the wasp had a wart on his nose,
Walter's wife Wanda walked on her toes.
Walter's son, Wally, wandered *away*!
And squandered his money on squabbling and play.

iii. I wonder what work that worm will do
Before it gets swallowed or nipped in two.

O or U 20

It seems illogical that **O** is often used in words where the sound is **u**, as in *come, love, money*. The reason for this has been suggested by Otto Jespersen in his *Essentials of English Grammar.*
He writes:

'The simple vowel U was used for the short vowel as in *up, us, nut, full,* etc., and for the diphthong [iu] or [ju], frequent in French words like *duke, use, due, virtue,* but also found in native words, e.g. *Tuesday, hue, Stuart* (the same word as *steward*).

But at a time when angular writing was fashionable, it became usual to avoid the letter **U** in close proximity with the letters **N, M** and another **U (V, W),** where it was liable to cause ambiguity (five strokes might be interpreted *imi, inu, mu, um, uni, uui,* especially at a time when no dot was written over *i*); hence the use of **O** which has been retained in a great many words: *monk, money, honey, come, won, wonder, cover* (written *couer* before V and U were distinguished,) *love,* etc.

A merely orthographic distinction is made between *son* and *sun, some,* and *sum*.'

DAYS OF THE WEEK

The days of the week are named after the gods worshipped in olden times. The spelling of the days is made easier by understanding their derivation.

Sunday:	people worshipped the sun.
Monday:	the moon was worshipped. It used to be Moonday. (A month is a *moonth,* the period of the moon's revolution.)
Tuesday:	named after a god of war, Tue. It was Tue's day.
Wednesday:	named after the god Woden. This was Woden's day, which accounts for the fact that there are 3 syllables in the modern spelling.
Thursday:	named after the god of thunder, Thor. It was Thor's day.
Friday:	people worshipped Freia, the goddess of beauty.
Saturday:	Saturn, the ancient Roman god of agriculture, was worshipped.

Pupils will be helped if it is pointed out that:

a. There are two days with *ur* in the spelling. They will then avoid using *er* or *ir* in Thursday and Saturday.

b. Tuesday, Wednesday and Thursday are days after gods of those names. The S at the end of their names denotes possession. Mistakes, such as Tuseday, will then be avoided.

HELPFUL HINTS:

Helpful Hint: *the*-words   Question words —
                     then   *whe*n
                     them   *whe*re
                     they   *wh*y
                     their   *wh*at
                     *the*re   *whi*ch
                                          *wh*o

Helpful Hint: **U**-tu*r*n

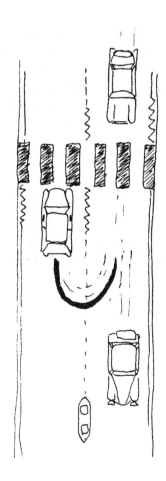

HELPFUL HINTS

Helpful Hint: *Al wal*ked and *tal*ked about ch*al*k on st*al*ks.

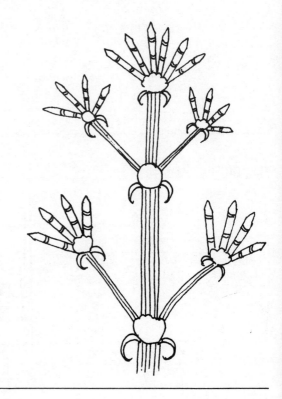

Helpful Hint: It's gr*eat* to *eat!*

HELPFUL HINTS

Helpful Hint: A *bus* is *busy*.

Helpful Hint: **U** and **I** b**ui**ld a house.

HELPFUL HINTS

Helpful Hint: *You* are *you*ng!

Helpful Hint: One autu*mn* day a colu*mn* of conde*mn*ed prisoners sole*mn*ly marched along singing hy*mn*s. "Da*mn*!" said the warder.

HELPFUL HINTS

Helpful Hint:
The *kn*ight *kn*ocked the *kn*ave on his *kn*uckles with a *kn*otted *kn*ob.
He *kn*ew when he *kn*elt on his *kn*ees, he had a *kn*ife in his *kn*itted *kn*ickers.

West Country Mnemonic: Oh! You be (**O U B**) *double* tro*uble*!

THE ENGLISH LANGUAGE

Teachers are often asked such questions as "Why is English spelling so illogical?", "Why are there so many words with the same meaning?" and even, "Why do we have to write at all?" The reason for the apparently irrational spelling is to be found in the history of the language, which is complex. Here are answers to some questions:

"Why is English spelling so illogical?"

The spelling is not so illogical as it first appears. The English language of today is a mixture of a number of languages, and the original spelling in each of these languages was very nearly phonetic.

The spelling guides in this book enable a person to understand more about the structure of words, and so realise that our spelling is for the most part logical.

"Why is English a mixture of languages?"

At various times in the early part of our history people from the continent of Europe invaded, and then settled in, the British Isles. The language that we now speak is a mixture of all their languages—in the same way that our nation is a mixture of all those peoples.

"Who were these invaders?"

The Romans In 55 B.C. Julius Caesar and his legions crossed the Channel and arrived in Britain, where tribes in the south-east of the country called the Belgae, were helping those Belgae still in Gaul to resist the Roman occupation. This time the Romans did not stay.

However, in 43 A.D. the Romans returned and in due course conquered most of the land, eventually settling here. Latin, the language of the Romans, was then spoken alongside Celtic, which was the language of the people already living here.

The Romans occupied this country for 400 years. The Celts were impressed by the Roman way of life and, when referring to it, no doubt used Latin terms. For instance, when veteran Roman soldiers were given land and settled down permanently with their families, they

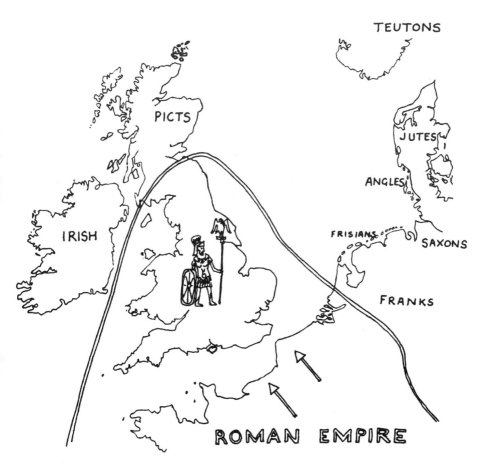

TEUTONS

PICTS

JUTES

ANGLES

IRISH

FRISIANS

SAXONS

FRANKS

ROMAN EMPIRE

would build a Roman *villa.* As time went on, the family multiplied and the settlement became known as a *village.* In feudal times serfs working on the land of the villa—by then known as the manor—were called *villeins,* from the Latin word, *villanus,* a farm servant. Later in our history the term became one of abuse—villain.

In the fifth century the Roman legions were recalled to Rome to defend their homeland which was being attacked by invaders from eastern Europe. This left Britain—a fertile land with few inhabitants—more or less defenceless.

THE ENGLISH LANGUAGE

The Anglo-Saxons Tribes in Frisia, North Germany and Denmark heard that there was good farming land in Britain and that the Roman legions had departed. These tribes—the Frisians, the Saxons, the Angles and the Jutes—invaded and settled in the eastern part of the country.

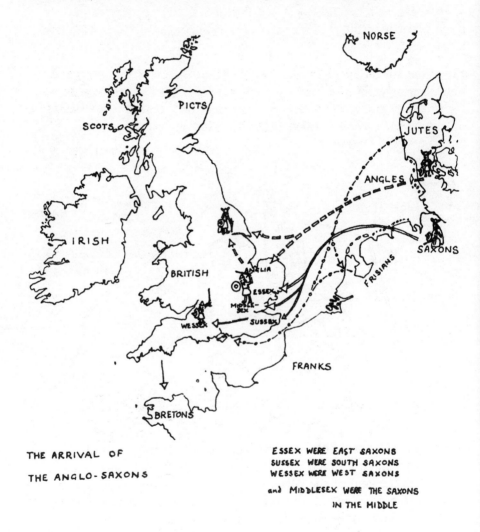

THE ARRIVAL OF

THE ANGLO-SAXONS

ESSEX WERE EAST SAXONS
SUSSEX WERE SOUTH SAXONS
WESSEX WERE WEST SAXONS

and MIDDLESEX WERE THE SAXONS
IN THE MIDDLE

They brought with them their own languages; the main ones were Anglian and West-Saxon—hence Anglo-Saxon or Old English. Celtic languages survived only in the western parts of Britain—in Cornwall, Wales, the Isle of Man, Ireland and Scotland.

THE ENGLISH LANGUAGE

The Vikings   About 800 A.D. the Vikings from the lands now known as Norway and Denmark raided the shores of Britain. Eventually they made settlements, first along the coasts and later inland. They were prevented from overrunning the whole country by Alfred, King of Wessex. He made a treaty with the Danish Vikings which permitted them to settle in the land known as Danelaw, in the north-eastern half of England.

Norse was the language of the Vikings. Some words used in present-day English which can be attributed to Norse are *knife, hut, stool, sofa* (originally meaning *the bench that one slept on*), as well as the names of towns that end in *by*, such as Derby, Whitby, Grimsby, for *by* means *town* in Danish.

AREAS OF VIKING

SETTLEMENT IN BRITAIN

IRISH

DANELAW

WELSH

WESSEX

THE ENGLISH LANGUAGE

The Normans In 1066 A.D. the Normans (i.e. *Northmen*, descendants
of Vikings from the North who had settled in northern France)
conquered all but Wales and Scotland. William of Normandy ruled the
country, and French was spoken at Court and amongst the aristocracy
until the thirteenth century. French was the official language,[1] and
it was not until 1363 that Parliament was opened once again in
English—for the first time since 1066. After that, the number of
French-speaking people in the land dwindled, though the upper
classes continued to use a considerable number of French words.
Therefore, in our language today French-derived words often
refer to a cultured environment, much of which has now become part
of our everyday life— *table, chair, mirror, library,* as well as *palace,
mansion, manor, estate, duke, marquess* and *viscount.*

This concentration of so many tongues in a comparatively small
geographical area[2] in time produced one language. It is both rich
and beautiful. Shades and subtleties of meaning can be conveyed,
impossible in most others. It is a particularly flexible language which
through the centuries has been adapted to the daily needs of many
peoples throughout the world.

"How did our one language emerge?"

All these languages, unevenly distributed throughout the land, resulted
in the development of various dialects. By the time Caxton set up his
printing press in Westminster in 1477, "the number of dialects [was]
almost as numerous as the counties of England, and moreover they were
perpetually changing. The Northerner, the West countryman, even the
housewife of Kent . . . could not easily understand either the London
merchant or one another".[3] (This, of course, is still sometimes the case
today.) The general acceptance of the speech of London and the Court
was encouraged first by Chaucer in his choice of dialect when writing
his *Canterbury Tales,* and then by Caxton who made the same choice
when printing, and lastly, through the Bible and Prayer Book, printed
copies of which were distributed throughout the country in Tudor times.

"When did spelling become standardised?'

Spelling used to be a matter of individual preference. People wrote down,
as nearly as they could with the symbols of our alphabet, the sounds

48 [1] For this reason many of our legal terms stem from French. The Church and the
learned professions generally have been even more profoundly influenced by Latin,
especially at the time of the Renaissance.

THE ENGLISH LANGUAGE

they heard. (See below.)

In the middle of the eighteenth century there was a movement towards generally acceptable forms of spelling. Dr. Johnson in 1755 produced the first dictionary and this set the standard for English orthography. At about this time correct spelling began to be an important concern of educated people.

"How did we get our alphabet?"

Early man drew pictographs to represent objects by pictures or symbols. These were later followed by ideographs which represented *ideas* through pictures of objects. Later still in man's development the *sounds* of language were represented by symbols. The full story is extremely complicated, but the Semitic languages played an important role in making spelling phonetical. The symbols used became known later as the *alphabet*. This word is a combination of the Greek letter-names *alpha* and *beta*—originally aleph (ox) and beth (house) in the Semitic— and corresponds to our ABC.

Greek letter-names were an adaptation of the Semitic. The original Semitic names are thought to be mnemonics for the letter-sounds in much the same way as children today say "a for *apple,* b for *bus,* c for *cat* "etc. The alphabet consequently took the equivalent form of *apple, bus, cat,* and so on. The letter-shapes were symbols for the objects.

The Greek letters were adopted and adapted by the Etruscans (from the area now known as Tuscany in Italy) and later modified by the Romans to form what we now call the Latin alphabet.

As Rome was the centre of Catholic Christianity, the Latin alphabet was used for religious writings which were copied throughout Western Europe. It then became the alphabet of Western European languages, always modified to meet the phonetic needs of each. The lower-case letters were developed for the purpose of cursive or joined-up script.

In English the (now) 26 symbols or letters have to cater for at least 40 sounds or phonemes. This can only be achieved by combining certain letters to represent other sounds. So, C and H, which separately

[2] Even today there are six languages spoken in these islands: Welsh, Scots Gaelic, Erse (Irish Gaelic), Manx, Cornish (being revived) and English.

[3] *English Social History* by G.M. Trevelyan, published by Longmans

have two distinct sounds, are put together–*ch*–to make a third sound. The same applies to *sh, th, ph, ng,* etc. The murmuring vowels– *ar, or, er, ir, ur,* –also provide additional sounds; so do the long vowels. In these ways the alphabet has been adapted to meet the needs of the English language. In French, for instance, accents and the cedilla have been employed to give certain letters a second or third sound, while in Scandinavian languages some vowel signs have been added– æ, ø and å. For every language symbols have been added or omitted as the need arose. But, it is still the same basic alphabet.

"What is meant by the structure of words?"

The structure of words is the way words are put together: prefix–stem– suffix. It is essential for bad spellers to understand this, for in this way they gain insight into how words are built up. Many people are surprised by the fact that prefixes and suffixes have meanings. These can be found in most dictionaries. When even a few of them are understood, many new words can be comprehended through analysis. This helps to improve comprehension of texts. However, the meanings of many words have become altered through the centuries, and their links with the original are not always immediately apparent. Dictionaries, especially dictionaries of etymology, can, of course, supply these links.

Here are some prefixes and suffixes:

Latin prefixes

(a) **AB**: from, away

abduct: to take away
absent: to be away
abstain: to keep oneself from
        (something)

(b) **AD**: to, towards

advance: move towards
advice: opinion (given) to (someone)

N.B. AD is often assimilated to the consonant following, facilitating pronunciation:

accept: ad/ac + cept: to take to
        oneself
allocate: ad/al + locate: to place
        (i.e. assign) to
arrest: ad/ar + rest: (i.e. bring) to a stop
approach: ad/ap + proach: (i.e. come)
        near to

(c) COM/CON: with, together

N.B. The first letter of the stem determines whether we write COM or CON, and this is directly related to ease of pronunciation.

complicate: *literally*, to twist together

congregate: to gather together

compare: to equal (i.e. measure) with

(d) PRO: before, in place of

proposition: that which is put before (someone)

pronoun: (i.e. a word) in place of a noun

(e) PER: through, thoroughly

perceive: to take in thoroughly

perfect: to make thoroughly

permit: to send (i.e. let) through

(f) RE: back, again

return: to turn back

regain: to gain again

(g) SUR: over

surprise: overtake (i.e. with something unexpected)

surcharge: a charge over (and above the basic)

(h) EX: out

exit: *literally*, it goes out (i.e. way out)

expel: drive out

(i) INTER: between

interrupt: to break in between

international: between nations

(j) EXTRA: outside, beyond

extraordinary: outside of the ordinary

extravagant: wandering beyond (the normal limits)

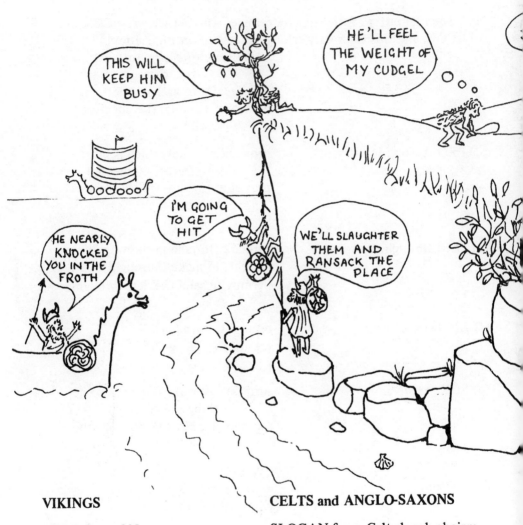

VIKINGS

NEAR from ON naer
KNOCK from ON knoka
FROTH from ON frotha
SLAUGHTER from ON slatr
RANSACK from ON rannsaka
HIT from ON hitta

ON = Old Norse

CELTS and ANGLO-SAXONS

SLOGAN from Celt sluagh-ghairm
BUSY from A-S bisig
WEIGHT from A-S (ge)wiht
CUDGEL from A-S cycgel
DIN from A-S dyne
SHUT from A-S scyttan

Celt = Celtic

ROMANS
DECAPITATE from L de + caput
VILLA from L villa
EXPECT from L expecto

FIGHT from A-S feohtan   JUST from L justus
STRIKE from A-S strican   FINISHED from L finis
NECK from A-S hnecca   SITUATE from L situs
CLOUT from A-S clut   CLIMATE from Gr klima
HEAD from A-S heafod   LETHAL from Gr lethe

A-S = Anglo-Saxon (Old English)   L = Latin   Gr = Greek

Latin suffixes

(a) ARY: belonging to,
      connected with

library: connected with books
missionary: belonging to a
        mission
revolutionary: belonging to a
        revolution

(b) ABLE/IBLE: able to, fit for

reasonable: able to be reasoned
readable: able to be read (i.e.
        subject matter)
legible: able to be read (i.e.
        deciphered)
edible: fit to eat

(c) OUS: full of

glorious: full of glory
joyous: full of joy
courageous: full of courage

Celtic prefix

A: on, in

away: on the way
aside: on the side
ashore: on the shore
asleep: in sleep

Greek prefixes

(a) TELE: far

telephone: sounds (words) from far
television: vision (sights) from far

(b) SYM, SYN: with, together

sympathy: feeling with (a person)
synchronize: to time together

THE ENGLISH LANGUAGE

Greek suffix

SCOPE: watcher, instrument
    for observing

telescope: instrument for ob-
    serving from afar
stethoscope: instrument for ob-
    serving (the chest)
horoscope: watcher of the hour
    (of a nativity)

Old English Suffix

SHIP: status, skill

friendship: status of being a friend
lordship: status of being a lord
seamanship: skill of being a seaman

The prefix—stem—suffix structure of words may be seen by taking the stem (root) of a word and building on to it. Interesting modifications may be observed in the process. Here are a few:

ped (Latin, *foot)*
*ped*al
im*ped*e
im*ped*iment
ex*ped*ition
ex*ped*ient
  *ped*igree
  *ped*icure
  *ped*estrian

*path*os (Greek, *feeling)*
a*path*y
  a*path*etic
sym*path*etic
sym*path*etically
unsym*path*etically
  em*path*y
  tele*path*y
  tele*path*ic

cap (Latin, *take)* — sometimes   *cep*
*cap*ture
*cap*tive
*cap*tivity
*cap*tivate
*cap*tivatingly
en*cap*ture
re*cap*ture

ac*ce*pt
ac*cep*tance
ac*cep*table
unac*cep*table
de*cep*tion
re*cep*tion
unre*cep*tive

ject (Latin, *throw*)
abject
abjectly
reject
rejection
projecting
dejected
objectionable
objectively
subject
injection
adjective
projectile
projector

mit, miss (Latin, *send*)
admit
admission
admittance
admittedly
submit
submission
dismissal
committee
remittance
missile
permission
mission
missionary
emission

ven, vent (Latin, *come*)
advent
adventure
convent
conventional
unconventionally

taka (Old Norse, *take*)
takes
overtaken
undertaker
intake
partaking (i.e. part taking
or taking part)

In many words prefixes and suffixes are linked to stems derived from other sources, typifying the intermingling of the original languages in our present-day English. The following are examples:

dis(L.) — *like*(O.E.) — *able*(L.)
over(O.E.) — *simplify*(L.) — *ing*(O.E.)
un(O.E.) — *sympathetic*(Gk.) — *al*(L.) — *ly*(O.E.)
un(O.E.) — *mis*(O.E.) — *take*(O.N.) — *able*(L.)

CONCLUSION

As far back as 1750 Lord Chesterfield wrote to his son as follows:

'I must tell you that orthography, in the true sense of the word is so absolutely necessary for a man of letters, or a gentleman, that one false spelling may fix a ridicule upon him for the rest of his life. And I know a man of quality who never recovered the ridicule of having spelled *wholesome* without the w.'[1]

Such an attitude towards mis-spellings, though not so harsh, has continued right up to the present time. Bad spelling is considered, often quite wrongly, to be a sign of lack of intelligence, and it is sniggered at by those able to spell with ease.

On the other hand, there is now a trend among the young to disregard standard spelling. This takes no account of the development of the language, and is merely a striving for the unconventional. With the increase, over the centuries, of written communication throughout the country—through the postal service, the need for official forms, etc.—standardised spelling has become important. One cannot put the clock back and once again make spelling a matter of individual choice.

However, common sense must prevail. Although attention should be given to accurate spelling, teachers must turn to adequate methods of instruction for those who are bad spellers because of poor perception for symbols. It should not be assumed automatically that a person with spelling problems is stupid, any more than one who cannot sing in tune. We do not all learn in the same way, and this should be borne in mind. Each person has his own perceptual strengths and weaknesses in the same way that each has different physical abilities. A multi-sensory approach to spelling difficulties will ensure that a pupil builds on his stronger abilities and is trained in his weaker ones.

The corollary of improved spelling is improved writing. This implies an understanding of grammar. The word *grammar* may bring to mind school-books containing dull exercises. In fact, grammar is the structure of spoken language, as well as of written. It is the essential difference between animal noises which communicate basic needs—such as hunger and fear—and the very complex communication of ideas between people. Each language has its own grammar. There is English grammar, French grammar, Japanese grammar, Swahili

[1] *English Social History* by G.M. Trevelyan, published by Longmans

CONCLUSION

grammar, etc. The way sentences are formed varies from one language to another, and this is one of the main reasons why it is impossible to translate one language into another word for word.

It is the grammatical structure of a language which enables a person to communicate clearly and precisely to others whatever ideas he may have—in much the same way as the mechanical structure of a car enables a driver to handle it with precision. In the same way that each model of car has its own mechanical peculiarities, so each language has its own special grammatical constructions or *conventions* which are generally accepted amongst its speakers. Without these conventions dialogue would be incomprehensible.

Spoken language preceded written language in man's evolution. Likewise, in the development of children, the ability to speak precedes the ability to write. Children learn early in life to reinforce spoken language by modulating the voice. Speech is also supported by facial expressions and hand gestures. Written language, however, has to be interpreted without the writer being present. He cannot break in with, "No! I didn't mean that, I meant such-and-such". Most of what is written has to bridge the gaps of time and space. Therefore, clarity of meaning in anything written is of the utmost importance. Even people with a great gift for writing are constantly improving their use of language in order to gain greater *clarity* of expression. Any author will have made several drafts of his work before he is satisfied that he has conveyed his meaning accurately to the reader. In the process, language becomes refined—in the true sense of the word!

For the pupil who is in the early stages of creating his own style of writing, there are two guides well worth noting. The first is to keep asking, "*Exactly what* am I trying to say?". And the second is to state it simply and clearly. Long words and complicated sentences do not necessarily make good writing. One writes in order to convey ideas to a reader, who should be enabled to grasp them without undue effort. This is, after all, good manners. For, to wrap up information in verbose terms usually indicates that the writer is more concerned with trying to impress, than with passing on useful and interesting information to the reader.

It is usually the most learned people in any nation who set the highest standards in both writing and speaking, expressing their opinions

CONCLUSION

lucidly and concisely. They extend the scope of their language in order to advance their ideas. However, we *all* influence the evolution of our mother-tongue. Every generation devises new words and expressions; some of these do not survive the passage of time, others become incorporated into our language and enrich it. Each one of us uses his mother-tongue in his own characteristic way. We mould it to express our personal needs and ideas. In this way English has developed through the ages and is a precious gift from our ancestors.

There is a great onus on teachers to give their pupils information on the structure and derivation of words, as well as to help them to express their ideas simply and clearly. (The importance of correct spelling in this process has been emphasised throughout this book.) In this way they will gain insight into the language which they are using daily; they will learn to use it effectively, and perhaps also enrich it for the enjoyment of others.

Suggestions for further reading

Growth and Structure of the English Language by Otto Jespersen,
published by Basil Blackwell

Essentials of English Grammar by Otto Jespersen,
published by George Allen & Unwin

Grammar by Frank Palmer, published by Penguin Books

The Languages of the British Isles Past and Present by W.B. Lockwood,
published by Andre Deutsch

Our Language by Simeon Potter published by Penguin Books

Place Names of the English-Speaking World by C.M. Matthews,
published by Weidenfeld & Nicolson

The Dyslexia Series: *Introduction—A Dyslexic's Eye-View*
by Helen Arkell

The Problem of Reading by Joy Pollock

The Problem of Spelling by Joy Pollock

The Problem of Handwriting by Elisabeth Waller

The Problems of Sequencing and Orientation by
Joy Pollock and Elisabeth Waller

The Importance of Motivation
by Adrienne Ackerman

Speech Therapy and the Dyslexic
by Daphne Hamilton Fairley

Books for the Dyslexic by Margaret Lulham
published by the Helen Arkell Dyslexia Centre

The Dyslexic Child by T.R. Miles, published by Priory Press

The Penguin Atlas of Ancient History by Colin McEvedy
published by Penguin Books

The Penguin Atlas of Medieval History by Colin McEvedy
published by Penguin Books

Notes

The following pages are left blank so that the owner of this book may make notes of further interesting information.

Notes

Notes